WOOD-SPIRIT

Front cover photograph courtesy of Andrew Kitchen

Wood-*Spirit*
Celebrating Trees and Life and Spirituality in Verse
By J S Morey

These poems are works of fiction. Names, characters, places and incidents are a product of the author's imagination or are used fictitiously. Any resemblance to actual events, locales or persons, living or dead, is coincidental.

No part of this book may be used or reproduced in any manner whatsoever without written permission from the author except in the case of brief quotations embedded in critical articles or reviews.

First published in Great Britain 2022
ISBN: 9798370588983

Copyright © 2022 by John Morey; All rights reserved

The moral right of the author has been asserted.

Further reading:

The series 'Love should never be this hard':

Book 1: The Sign of the Rose
Book 2: The Black Rose of Blaby
Book 3: Rose: The Missing Years
Book 4: Finding Rose

Wild Hearts Roam Free – a modern western set in Wyoming
Unresolved? - a short story linked to 'Wild Hearts Roam Free'

Those Italian Girls – set in the hills of Tuscany

Read My Shorts – short stories and poems with a message

For more by this author
visit www.newnovel.co.uk

PREFACE

A life without trees is a life without... well... life, some would say.

The scientific fact that we need trees to live – to survive as a species – is undisputed. They provide the planet with oxygen.

But they represent more, spiritually. They feed our soul and, as a European living in a lush, green landscape, I feel privileged. We all should feel blessed, if we live in a land of trees.

Hence the title: Wood-*Spirit.*

This collection of thoughts in verse addresses trees themselves, the human race separately, and the partnership between trees and mankind. Within the title, 'woods' and 'trees' could be interchangeable, but 'woods' has been chosen because of the perception held by many that they contain a spiritual quality that may be as illusive as it is mysterious.

This will resonate immediately with those familiar with folk and fairy tales, but you don't need to be a scholar of either to sense a special presence as you move silently within woodland or forest.

Similarly there are those among you who say you connect with individual trees – those standing solus within a rural setting.

Hopefully you will connect with the following

and enjoy the experience in a similar fashion.

THE DEAD TREE

A tree has a value retained even after death - for those who live from, on, and in its remains. For some creatures they become a home; for others, a food source.

We also retain a value after we have departed this earth– for friends and family - not necessarily material wealth. Our real worth for those who survive us call them memories.

In both cases, the spirit lives on...

I am an old tree.
Dead. Some would say worthless,
(Apart from those deep within my domain
Who live among my impotent limbs.)

For some I am a permanent home;
Other residents see me as a convenience.
Within my bark they find refuge,
Shelter - even food -
For insects and small creatures.

What little remains of my branches
Provides a resting place.
Not permanence for the feathered
Or a place to bring up family -
Unless they should burrow deeper;

Deeper into my soul
To explore my lifeless trunk.
I may sprout green again
Even though merely grass,
Or weed. Sometimes bloom
Seeded in the dust and dirt
Collected after my death.

Those new shoots you see are not mine;
Nor are they my children.
Born of seed and borne by bird,
Or carried by the wind
I am merely their host.

I see myself in Man
As Man may see me in them -
In a world where the old and dead
Often leave a legacy.

If I do leave something behind
Then the recipient has few options
In deciding who benefits from my gifts;
Whether dead, or dying.

Some take little pieces from me,
Material or spiritual - on loan as it were.
Others win title and rights to me
To steel the inherited riches;
Taking them for their own purpose.

Ideally, there is a third way
Instead of plundering what is left:
To take and build on my bounty,
For the good of many.

Liken this to the axeman who,
Seeing my treasure, harvests it.
He may then secure my worth
For himself or for others,
Before decay sets in.

The alternative would be to disappear
Or for me to be taken without a care.
To be forgotten.

As for constant threats
From my all-time enemy -
Man –
Fire is what I fear most.

Now that constitutes a real loss.

~ *** ~

THE HAWTHORN

There are those who believe bringing hawthorn blossom into the house leads to illness and death, as well as saying that it is bad luck to cut down a hawthorn tree.

The Hawthorn is linked to a Gaelic festival celebrating spring, Beltane, on May 1st, for which armfuls of blossom would be gathered

In Celtic mythology it is a sacred trees symbolising love and protection - consistent with its reputation as a natural medicine for many conditions. Allegedly.

It is also referred to as the 'bride of the hedgerow'.

The young leaves are edible and, as children, we would refer to them as 'bread and cheese'.

> I am everywhere but usually ignored,
> Even though I offer a value for many.
>
> If only they would ask.
>
> In May, dewdrops from my leaves
> Can enhance a maiden's beauty,
> Or give craftsman's hands more skill.

WOOD-SPIRIT

Unlike the oak I lack stature so,
To compensate, I abound in number.
Sometimes I form a whole hedgerow.
That's where my berries attract attention,
Albeit mainly from birds.
For food.

But the wiley schoolboy is often first
To feast upon my bounty - my leaves.
In early Spring I am green and fresh,
A treat that many a child may use to tease
Their friends - with 'bread and cheese'.
(Or 'Bara Caws' the Welsh call it.)

In spite of earlier recognition of my worth,
Later, very few go on to use my berries
For preserves; Salads; Even wine.

Or most importantly - medicinally.

Maybe they should.

Among Man I have my equivalent.
Abundant. Everywhere.
Overshadowed by the vociferous;
By the bold; by the gregarious.
Even by the needy - for others.

Yes. My human counterpart exists aplenty.
Offering shade and shelter -
Even nourishment to those around.
(But more so gifts of the spiritual kind.)

However, like the larger tree, I am often cut;
Dispatched, replaced; or simply ignored.

I'm not sure which is the more unjust.

Therefore...
It's as well I have no real feelings,
Otherwise my burden from forming
That traitorous crown for The Lord
Would be much too great to bear.

~ *** ~

THE OAK

Next to the yew, the English oak is known for longevity.

As such a perennial part of the English landscape, alongside its myths and legends, it is part of what 'being English' stands for.

They say the oak built the British navy and, for that, we should give it credit for our sovereignty.

Even as more and more tree species from beyond our shores are introduced, so the oak remains protected and central to our landscape, whilst holding a special place in our hearts because of it.

Likewise, our own indigenous cultural values will hopefully survive; enriched by outside influence.

I am The Oak.
They often call me solid.
Some say I'm a symbol of the English
(Whether that's a good thing or not
Depends on what you think of the English!)

One thing is for certain:
I've been around as long as mankind
Or even longer. However...

Longevity is not necessarily a measure
Of strength, solidity - or value.
Unless you're the oak in question.

If I stand for anything at all, then
Consistency and the absence of change
Are reasons I have survived.
(When all around have flexed or failed.)

'Move with the times,' they say.
Some people move. Some change.
Some do so purely to survive.
Others mainly to thrive.

Once planted and mature I cannot move.
For centuries I face storm, flood, drought.
Or even Man himself, with his axe.

Man contends with similar threats,
Including the axe, wielded by a fellow!
(There are few 'axe suicides' by oaks.)

So, if I will not - cannot - move, therefore…
Do I not stand in the way of progress?

Maybe.
But only if I block your path.
(Which could take me years.)

The oak cannot learn from Man but
Is the reverse not possible?
At least the oak adapts to the seasons

As so should Man.
(Seasons being forces neither controls.)

And the oak is home for others -
Those who have their own value. To others.

Its branches offer both shade and shelter
From life's sunny and rainy days,
For both Man and beast.

Its leaves and those of it's arboreal cousins
Deliver the very essence of Life.
Oxygen.

Beyond that, the ability to change
And freedom to change and adapt,
Should be protected.

As should the right to remain unchanged.

The true gift is to know which is right.
How, when, and for whom.

~ *** ~

THE ROWAN

'Living on Dartmoor, the Rowan Tree was a familiar sight – its berries providing nourishment for birds, even in winter.

When cooked they proved useful and nutritious as jam or jelly (but poisonous to humans if uncooked), but it was hard to find anyone who did used them.

Few spoke of its spiritual properties, but its myths and legends *are* listed here...'

To keep you safe on your journey
(Whether travelling in mind or body)
You could do worse than carry
A stick made from Rowan.

But let that be the limit of your prunings -
To cut the red-headed down would be wrong,
Bringing bad luck and, perhaps, more grief.

Favoured especially by Gaelic and Norsemen -
Its strong, resilient qualities produce fine tools -
Handles for tools, spindles, and spinning wheels
For cloth – dyed by Celts using its bark and berries
For garments in their ceremonies.

And was it not the god Thor

Whose life the Rowan saved?
Stretching its branches to the extreme
It plucked that noble lord from a raging torrent
Lest he be swept downstream
Into the underworld - and lost.
Is it therefore not by chance
You rarely see the Rowan victim of lightning?

This Tree of Life offers courage, wisdom -
Protection from evil if planted near the home.

Along with Blackthorn, Hawthorn and Ash,
Rowan is regarded often as a Fairy Tree.
They - the fairies - live under Rowan trees
And ward off witchcraft and enchantment,
As may its berries.
Fairy or berries, or both, are guardians.
It's hard to judge which is stronger.

Like the Hawthorn or the Ash,
Rowan often stands alone in fields -
Sentried by a ring of stones
To signify they belong to the fairies.

Allegedly.

~ *** ~

THE SPIRIT OF THE WOODS

Woods and forests are birthplaces for many a myth, legend – and fairy tale. For those with a heightened sense of spirituality they present an eeriness and enchantment that is almost tangible.

Certainly, if ever we do experience connections that have such a profound effect on us at the time, inevitably they are ones that stay with us.

I am the spirit of the woods
Of the trees, living within their midst.
(Sometimes within their mist,
But then I'm really silent.)

Those who value me most
Know me as 'the woods':
A collection of trees to delight
Even the most un-impressionable
When the mood takes me.
Or my mood takes them.

But my influence is never so powerful
As to overwhelm - like my cousin, the forest.

Unlike that greater spirit
I spare comfort for smaller clan -
Badgers, foxes, birds of most feather
And, if I am lucky, deer.

WOOD-SPIRIT

(Oh, I do like deer!)

But let us not forget those who live
With - and for - those creatures:
Humble insect and smaller mammal.

Of course there is another; an element
Known only by touch and sound -
Sometimes by smell - but never by sight.
The wind.
Some say *he* is the spirit of the woods,
Altering the state of mind of all who enter.
But he cannot achieve this on his own.
He borrows from his friends, the trees -
Using their leaves in a variety of ways;
As instruments.

Breeze creates an almost inaudible rustle;
Whilst dapple of light filters through.
On another day, breeze may turn to gale,
Rage and strength combined so greatly
As to shred the messenger, those very same leaves.

I can be viewed from within or afar.
Affecting senses more than words.
Within, I can be your home, your playground,
Your moment of peace. Perhaps
your hiding place.

From without and afar I do but enhance
All that surrounds me,
Offering a welcome destination

For those who wish to visit.
All I ask is that you keep me safe and,
In turn, I will do my best for you.
I will provide all the above for you to enjoy
But, more than that, if you keep me well
Then I will deliver the very essence of life.

Take that as my promise to you.
My vow.

But should I suffer harm by your actions
Then what might follow bears no imagining,
Being beyond the control of any promise.

All this lies deep within my spirit;
The spirit of the woods.

~ *** ~

THE YEW TREE

In researching the background of the yew, what surprised me most was how long they have lived.

For instance, to sit under its boughs or lean against it, one cannot help but marvel that – for a tree that may number thousands of years – those who may also have 'sat and leant' all those centuries ago, could have been under the threat of The Plague or have been conscripted for the Holy Wars...

To label me 'the tree of death' seems unfair,
Given that I outlast most and many tree species,
Sometimes living for several thousand years.

In any case, I never intend to harm anyone.

One warning though (and this is serious):
All parts of me are poisonous to Man.

Animals and cattle don't fare well either
So keep away; keep your distance!

Man can live for a hundred years;
I have beaten that a thousand fold.

But to what end? For either of us?

It may only prove worthwhile
If we are blessed with good health,
With a good partner; with good friends.

(Oh, and good memories.)

At the end of a long life,
Who remembers what we do?
What have we learnt; what do we know?

For that matter, who else cares?

As one yew to another, I can explain
Why we seem to grace graveyards
In favour of other resting places.

We were planted by priests and reverends
To discourage sheep-owners and the like
Letting stock graze beneath our boughs.
I would kill them, you see,
Not by my act, but by their foolishness.

(Foolish enough to eat my leaves;
They are welcome to my berries.)

But ask yourself; 'why would men of God
Begrudge hungry livestock a free lunch?'
(And keep their graves tended for free?)

The longer living among my kind
Survived the plague.

WOOD-SPIRIT

Rumour has it that saplings were planted
ON graves to purify the interred.
Another reason? Or another myth?

Latterly, I have been used for weapons -
For the English Longbow.
But in peace-time for tool handles.

Such a contrast!
'Beating swords into ploughshares'
Is a trend I would wish for.

I am happy for other greenery
To surround me, but some desist.
The Willow prefers wet land
Whereas sodden soil would kill me.

And don't expect to see me near Cacti.
(For opposite reasons.)

I survive, although I wonder ' What if?
What if Christianity -
With its churches and graveyards -
Had failed? (Heaven fordid!)
What if there had never been a pandemic?

Or no simple minds with simple solutions,
Seeding yew trees to purify the dead?'

'Where would I have lived?
And what good would I do?'

Every tree has a purpose
And mine would be trivial...
Relegated to garden hedges, perhaps?
~ *** ~

TREES

I took a picture on one of our walks with grandchildren in Stover Park. This poem was born at that moment.

Stretched out on a bench, looking skywards, the textures and random patterns invoked a certain peace against the natural sounds of the woods.

With three trillion trees on the planet
And 400 trees for every living human being,
'Surely there must be enough to go round'
(I hear you say.)

It's true. For now. Maybe.
But for how long? ... in any case
I am not here to lecture you
On the worth of trees.
There are others more qualified than I
And you probably don't need telling.

I am here to discuss something much more...
More compelling. Something or someone.
You, perhaps. Or 'us'. Man.

Consider this:
To begin with trees have roots.

They spread not far from the centre.
Not far from the trunk -
Matched by equal radius above ground.
Matched by branches.

Is that not the same for you and I?
When we were young, our roots, experiences,
Grew downwards for stability.
But not so much outwards for knowledge.
That came later for most. Hopefully.
We are nourished – nurtured – by parents
(Again, hopefully!)
In the same way rainfall and minerals
Feed the tree through its roots.
(Or in our case by family influence
But not always our own.)

But what of branches?
Are they not a visible sign of growth?
Of progress, however modest?
They blossom with flower, leaf and fruit.
Initially this is a poor display
Compared with what is to come
As trees grow with each season and ring.

Are we, Man, not the same?
Consider the tree whose visible signs
Show poorly against it's neighbours. Its peers.
Is it a consequence of a poor root system?

How will we find answers without digging
Deeper into the root system of either -

WOOD-SPIRIT

Of tree, or of person? Man?

More to the point, does anyone care?
Perhaps we should care,
Otherwise, there lies a danger.

'There but for the grace of me do you live.
Exist, Survive, Thrive.'
(Says the woodsman with his axe.)

'There but for the grace of me do you go,
Breathe. Grow. Prosper.'
(Says the tree with its roots,
Branches. Leaves. Flowers. Fruit.)

… but most importantly with its oxygen
Empowering us from its passive soul.

~ *** ~

THE WILLOW TREE

The Weeping Willow is native to China and is associated with many mystical powers and properties. The goddess of compassion – Kuan Yin – is linked with the willow. The shape of its leaves is said to equate to the tears she sheds for human suffering.

The image of the willow is our path to hope, healing and stability. It also is said to provide us with a sense of belonging and safety.

> Man identifies himself with me
> Or, at least, claims we share the notion
> That my cascading leaves and branches
> Match his tears.
>
> For that, I may be called 'Weeping Willow'.
>
> But I also heal and ease the pain of Man
> Both mental and physical.
>
> As for my name it's a fair choice, I guess.
> After all I have seen my share of woe;
> Man's woes he has shared with me.
>
> Living by water I have seen drownings
> Of man, animal; sometimes both.

(Where one tried to save the other but failed.)
Man differs from the rest of God's creatures.
That difference is caring. Empathy.
Or lack of it.
Caring enough to save the fallen.
(In the above case, the fallen in!)

Man saving man is seen as compassion,
Or love. Or both.

Man saving animal - much the same,
But self-service may decide if and when.

If I am not found living by river or stream
Then I tap into the water below me,
Seeking groundwater rather than aquifer.

That said,
It's open, passing waters that grant me wisdom.
I lift my own dreams from their freedom
Deep within their endless journey.

Then there are my visual qualities.

The sight to savour is the wind in my leaves
Like maiden's tresses caught in a storm.

Otherwise, watch for my own slender branches
Reaching into running water. And ask.
'Do the swirling pools try to cling on
In the vain hope of carrying them away
Were they not attached?'

You may ask 'Am I used for furniture?'
Sometimes.
More commonly I will be woven
For a fence or hurdle for animals.
But, in spite of what they say,
Rarely for a cricket bat.

(Thankfully, even rarer for a coffin!)

I am found in generous space
In rows - but not as a hedge.
Gardens, too, but never as wood or forest.
Not exclusively in its entirety,
But nestled within arboreal cousins.
(Not prejudging the company I keep.)

Ornamental, I may also be,
But more practical and life-giving
For the many insects and tiny animals;
Tenants who call me 'home'.

They are my true companions.
And the only ones who weep,
Sad when I am gone.

~ *** ~

A STORY OF TREES

It was one of those bright sunny days when Jane and I were only too happy to have the grandchildren for the day.

Our picnic was simple - prepared and packed in a matter of minutes. We were soon in the heart of Dartmoor, at Holne Bridge (or New Bridge, it's one and the same.)

We soon found a quiet spot a few yards along the river, a short distance from the car. Our girls are usually not too noisy, which was just as well as there was a group of five girls of perhaps 20-something close by, but out of ear-shot.

They were meditating.

It was easy to see why as, surrounded by trees with the only other sound being that of running water, the setting was perfect.

Little wonder trees have such a spiritual presence.

THE BEECH TREE

If the oak is the king of the woodland
Then Mother Beech is the queen.

Perhaps he sought her protection and good fortune,
Just as she was attracted to his strength.
Or possibly it's the wisdom the beech presents.
True, she - the beech - gave us the first book.
Or 'boc', as the Anglo-Saxon called them.
But who was first to write on strips of beech?
More so, what did he - or she - write?
And why?

On reflection, it was doubtless a cleric
Sharing 'his religion' with subscribers,
Introducing a heavenly significance
Fitting for this holiest of trees.

It must be true.
What proof do you need if, as they say,
To prayer under a beech tree
Connects you to heaven?

But should you find yourself lost
On a less spiritual journey then take heart.
The traveller seeking shelter under a beech
Shall survive the night free from harm.

I assume someone has tested this theory,
But what better way to extend good fortune
Than to wear pieces of this noble tree
As a good luck charm for a safe passage?

You may even decide to go further.
Some say that, if you scratch a wish
Upon a piece of beech and bury it,
Good fortune could follow.

Nor is it by chance the beech
Inspired the building of cathedrals.

Appropriate - if it nurtures open minds,

Encouraging tolerance and sympathy -
Not to mention a better future
When used for healing and meditation.

Perhaps it should also be named
'The thinking man's tree'.

~ *** ~

THE SYCAMORE

As youngsters, we rarely looked beyond the 'helicopters' raining down on us on a windy day after school.

When asked to draw a tree leaf it would usually be the sycamore we remembered and, on a hot summer's day, outside, the one tree we could count on to provide shade.

Nothing beats the sight of a single sycamore standing solitary in a vast meadow - winter or summer.

I am yet another another sacred tree;
A symbol of strength, protection,
Eternity, Fertility and Divinity.

Should you care to use my mighty limbs
To scale and therefore gain a better view
Of friend approaching, or of enemy,
Even a better vision of life itself -
Your surroundings -
I will carry your weight confidently.

Tax collectors have been known
To climb my branches,
going to biblical lengths
to catch sight of The Lord.
Zack did so with some success and,
Once noticed, offered Him a night's stay
In return for his blessing.

(I have this on good authority.)

Since inception by Roman hand
Sycamore seeds have used air travel
To disperse themselves - Wind-bound
To self-propagate and to multiply.

I was also ahead of my time
When it came to aviation invention.

Even before helicopters claimed credit
(Ignoring Michaelangelo for one moment)
Young boys had found great delight
In my seeds' aerial properties.

As for the seeds themselves? And leaves?

Steer clear of my poison within.
Those dangers are for all to see,
But what lies beneath?

It is sometimes said of all trees
Their roots go deeper than we know.
Seeking other roots, other trees

Communicate with each other; and...

Not with us, but about us?

If trees really *could* talk
(But then, who says they can't?)
The sycamore might say:

'Use me, but don't abuse me
Because you are always welcome
To my shade.

~ *** ~

THE SILVER BIRCH

On first noticing the silver birch, the initial question might be 'Why are you so different?'

Certainly, ancient cultures recognised it as symbolising new beginnings, and it is easy to see how it might be seen as a guardian of the weary or disoriented traveller through unfamiliar countryside.

Although hardy when growing, once fallen or felled, its fibres quickly disintegrate to become the home for earth-borne creatures, whilst other birches continue their rapid growth skyward.

A colourful resident in any wood or forest.

I am the white lady of the forest.
Ancients once called me Berchta,
But I am associated with other deities.
Some say I have eyes which,
With my white form, I can guide you
Safely on your perilous journey
Across hills and mountains; safely home.

Protection is just one gift I offer
Together with rebirth and purification.
For those reasons I am considered sacred.

Tolerance to hard climes helps me to survive.

I grow quickly - but I'm fortunate if I age -
Happy merely to become a centenarian.

Many love me for my looks alone -
My bark and my golden leaf of autumn.
I prefer to be known for richer qualities,
Those that embrace the spiritual.

Frost has you swinging from my branches.
(Thanks for that, Robert.)
But I am rarely used for climbing by children,
My branches being too slender.
Although sunlight dapples freely.
Blessing those below.

THE SPINNEY

The spinney - aka copse - is often used as a refuge by, and for, game birds - often sited within the larger expanse of a field in an estate or farm.

As with nature in general, the spinney can expand, grow, mature - even with or without the introduction of additional tree species.

Whilst all the time retaining a mystical presence.

One prize I recall as a boy was to venture into a spinney in search of...? Who knows? The unknown.

Imagine my delight when I discovered an apple tree, hidden away from other eyes - so far. I knew this because every branch abounded in fruit.

The first time. On my second visit a week later, it had been stripped. And not by fairies!

The SPINNEY

She looked up at me expectantly:
'We *are* going out? *Aren't* we?'
How could I ignore that look,
Those eyes full of love, trust,
Companionship, too?

Bess was a short-haired Collie
Crossed with...? We never knew.
She was useless with sheep.
Just as well we had none.

But Bess was better than geese
When it came to farm security.
Less messy, too; Indoors.
We began our Sunday ritual;
Our weekly treat to each other
After the pub; after lunch.
It was our walk together before dark.
'Bring a seasoned log back with you,'
Was Dad's final instruction.
We left the warmth of the kitchen
With an extra mission, now.

The kitchen stove never went out
But fuel was low; seasoned fuel, that is.
The cold snap of early winter
Had eaten into our reserves.
Normally we took tractor and trailer
Collecting firewood. And earlier.

But other tasks - essentials -
Had come first last summer.
Now bad weather threatened,
Prioritising our next task.

Once released Bess raced ahead,
Pointing to the spinney.

She had made a good choice.

Should we be fortunate
To stumble upon ash branches -
Even those fallen, still green -
They could still count as firewood
For immediate burning.

We both loved the spinney
For its hidden secrets.
Fur and feather - game or feral -
Peering from bramble or thicket
But rarely seen; seldom heard.
At least by me; but maybe by Bess.
But then there was the invisible -
The eyes of a spiritual kind.
Like me, did she notice them, too?

My thoughts drifted to former times;
To summer when she was still with me.
She?
I mean Emily, now, not Bess.
The spinney held special secrets.
Ours. Emily's and mine.
Bess remained close; always watching.

The clearing in the spinney centre
Was our favourite place.
We were headed there now,
To check what memories remained.
We? Just Bess and I.
Not Emily.

She was gone, but the memories?
They would never leave.
One thing of ours, hers and mine,
She couldn't take from me;
But she could take them with her.

Did she recall every single moment
As fondly as I now did? But alone?
And as painfully?
It was pain I couldn't do without.
If she felt the same pain too,
Could it be greater than mine?
I doubted it.

Her reason for leaving was simple:
I had become so close, I stifled her.
She *had* to leave. To escape.
It's a cliche, but they do say:
'Grip sand too tightly and the grains
Will slip through your fingers.'
(I will refrain from saying it, but:
'Life really is a beach'.)

I held her too tightly (In spirit, that is).
So she slipped through.
Was it an escape? If so to where?
More especially, to whom?

Hopefully to no-one; no-one I know.

Such fragile thoughts held me,
Held my reasoning captive

Until we reached the spinney.
Bess raced straight to the clearing.
Our clearing.
The afternoon sun was warm,
Finding its way easily through -
Through a thin canopy of leaves.

Were they birches? Or ash?
It didn't matter which.
Sun strength was all that mattered.

Bess found the bank;
Our own grassy bank -
First mine and Emily's;
Now a retreat for Bess and me.

We sat for hours, Emily and I,
Me - reading, she - listening,
When she wasn't sleeping.
I would let her sleep
Solely so I could watch her;
Watch her and imagine.
Imagine what she was thinking;
Dreaming. Escaping?

I hoped it was to dream - of me
(In a good way, of course).
If not - then something happy;
Happy thoughts - again, of me.

Then all that changed. Was lost.
I pondered on our final days often:

Was losing Emily *to a rival*
Easier than to no-one?
If so, then he was tangible;
Comparable; Visible. Real.
She was certainly real then.
But...
Looking down at the emptiness
Below me where she once lay,
She is no less real.
Not even now.

Now I have to be content
With the eyes of my Bess
Looking up at me.

No matter how much I care,
How much I squeeze the sand
That represents our love
For each other, Bess and I,
Our grains will never run out.

Just as secrets of the spinney live on,
So our feelings will never die,
If only in ny imaginings. And hers?

Emily was the last to come
And the first to leave in my life.
The same is said of the ash,
The Kings Tree - a life force.
Ash is a renewing spiritual presence
Comprising a third of these woods.

So, dear ash, with all your medicines
Will you heal my ills and weaknesses,
Albeit those of a romantic nature?
Is all that within your remit?

If so, then may I take one limb,
Just one for now, for firewood,
Green though it may be
And recently fallen, not felled?

Later, as I watch you burn
(Your sacrifice for my warmth,
And my mental wellbeing),
Can my painful memories dissolve?
Burn with you - to disintegrate
Before disappearing heaven-bound
To be drawn upon later - possibly -
Should ever I be in need of you?

Perhaps in prayer?

~ *** ~

THE ALDER

From insect repellent to easing rheumatism, the alder has been linked with many a natural remedy - mental as well as physical.

But I will leave you to seek expert advice on that one - I am no doctor.

Without doubt it has been valued over the centuries, even though now it rarely receives a mention for any of its qualities, as a building material or otherwise.

>Was there ever a tree living
>Without mystical properties,
>Then I have yet to hear of it.
>
>The alder is no exception.
>
>Back in the day, the mighty warrior
>Preferred a shield made of alder
>Confident it would keep him safe,
>And bleed red instead of him, if struck.
>
>The alder loves the treacherous bog
>And water, to grow and thrive.
>
>For that reason the unwary traveller

Would be wise to avoid and not pass.
Not too close, at least.

This love of water makes alder strong,
A soaking renders it as hard as iron
Without degrading if submerged.

Venice is built on alder piles.
Venice will never rot.

Amsterdam, too, has alder foundations
But goes one usage further -
To shoe its nation in clogs!

There may be only slender truth
That alder formed the first Man
(With Rowan producing Woman).
It shows pioneer spirit another way,
Being the first to reclaim
The clearing in a forest.

Talking of spirits, could it be true
That fairies' clothes are dyed
With alder to render them invisible?

And can a whistle made from alder
Summon the wind and water nymph?

There is no doubt alder loves water.
Even its catkins are water-borne,
Floating downstream, coming ashore
To germinate and thrive -

For up to a century and a half.

There it enriches its surroundings
With fertile soil for its neighbours.

If ever a tree were truly loved
For its service to others,
The alder would rank high.

~ *** ~

THE HOLLY

The holly tree - or bush - is associated either with good (usually fairies) or evil (the devil).

Years ago I lived on Dartmoor. When the farmer was hedgelaying I asked why he left the holly untouched, still above the line of finely crafted hawthorn and other trees.

"That's where the Devil lives," was his reply.

A similar thing happened much later when I was cutting back a holly that had invaded the decking. My neighbour was careful to point out that I should save some sprigs - which he then took - on the basis that he was taking the fairies with him, to his garden and a new home.

Green and strong through winter,
Holly is a reminder that nature
(Principally indigenous birdlife)
Needs sustenance year round.
They rely on its rich larder;
Its bright red berries.

One friend - neighbour - told me
How he brought holly indooors
Laden with fairies, in winter,

To keep them warm.

They provided *him* warmth too
Of a spiritual kind.
(Or so he said, keeping him safe)

And he was a church-goer!

Speaking of the protective qualities
Of holly - and Dartmoor (Widecombe) -
I wonder if the church yard there
Has holly growing within.
Some say holly wards off lightning
Such as the strike on its tower
Centuries past by the Evil One.

Perhaps someone should check.

Others say holly is good firewood
Even burnt green (better a year later).
Again, should we not take care
If cutting for the hearth,
To leave some ready to grow again

You can never be too sure.

~ *** ~

THE LARCH

Although associated with evergreens such as pine, the larch is unique in that it sheds its fine leaves in winter.

A softwood, it is sufficiently strong and resilient for cladding and other timber uses, whilst other sources are quick to point out the dangers of its high resin content.

It is also reported to have edible qualities in its bark, you may have to travel a long distance to find anyone who includes larch in their larder.

As always, take expert advice, not hearsay.

Is nothing else said of the larch
Other than 'It's good for firewood?'

(This generous and forgiving tree
Even thrives best in cooler climes
Where warm homes and dry wood
Are most appreciated.)

If that were not enough
Its bark is said capable of nourishing us

Medicinally and for breadmaking.

(But I would check first;
Seek expert advice before trying.)

Safer, therefore, to limit its use
To timber and to building,
Relying on its hardiness
To construct the home.

Better still…
Leave it undisturbed
For birdlife and squirrels
To enjoy its food and shelter.

~ *** ~

COPSE AND ROBBERS

There was something special to be said about sneaking around a copse as a young boy - especially when you knew you weren't supposed to be there!

Skulking across a vast open field in order to reach the secrecy and seclusion of dense woodland only adds to the excitement.

No wonder so much local folklore - magic and mystery - surrounds these supposedly haunted domains.

The same can be said of the cliffs, caves and tunnels associated with our coastal regions - especially those places favoured by smugglers of old.

There's a clear similary between the latter and poaching, in that both were (and still are!) considered illegal, albeit a necessary pastime for the less fortunate.

> Coasts have smugglers, wreckers too,
> Keeping our lawmen busy.
> But step inland for contraband;
> Such trade is equally privy:

Poaching.

Both haunt the night so you'll take fright
From their missions quite illicit.
Don't venture near in case you hear
Their motives - too explicit.

They haunt you see, every tree
And cave along the shore.
Those they serve (for hors d'oeuvre)
Keep coming back for more.

Smuggling is a special trade
Passed on from dad to son.
Poaching, too, sports fair game
That's prized by everyone.

They often boast that ghoul and ghost
Threaten, in every sound.
It keeps them safe from Lord or waif
Whether unarmed, or with hound.

Woods are where I have my lair
To keep my trade alive.
I set my traps with snares in gaps
Till feather or fur arrives.

But I need to keep all traces
Of my less than legal wares,
Away from prying eyes and ears,
With secret threat that scares.

So keep your walks deep in my woods
Confined to daytime hours.
Or else I'll have to consult my muse
Invoking harmful powers.

~ *** ~

FINAL WORDS FROM AUTHOR J.S. MOREY

I hope these poems encourage you to explore nature in a new light – and more often.

Please always respect the code of the countryside – and take extra care if foraging for nature's bounty in terms of fungi, plants and berries – some of which may be delicious and nutritious, but many may be poisonous.

Keep children safe and take an expert with you if in any doubt regarding toxicity and edibility.

These poems also address the spiritual qualities of trees as expressed in cultural heritage, folklore, beliefs, myth and legend.

It is left to the reader to decide what to believe. Any allusions in these verses are taken from sources voiced by others based on their background, belief system, or stories handed down over time.

They do not reflect the views of the author.

~ *** ~ * ~ *** ~

Printed in Dunstable, United Kingdom